D1124105

The science of a sprint
33305234619454
0jn   5/6/16

THE SCIENCE OF A SPRINT

ELLEN LABRECQUE

Published in the United States of America by Cherry Lake Publishing
Ann Arbor, Michigan
www.cherrylakepublishing.com

Content Adviser: Dr. Thomas Carroll, Associate Professor of Physics and Astronomy, Ursinus College
Reading Adviser: Marla Conn, ReadAbility, Inc.

Photo Credits: © Berc/iStock.com, cover, 1; © Andrey Yurlov/Shutterstock.com, 5; © Pete Niesen/Shutterstock.com, 6;
© Maxisport/Shutterstock.com, 7; © David Eulitt/ABACAUSA.COM/Newscom, 8; © nikolaich/Shutterstock Images, 11;
© Colman Lerner Gerardo/Shutterstock Images, 13; © Berc | Dreamstime.com - Sprinter Leaving Starting Blocks
Photo, 15; © MaxiSports | Dreamstime.com - Kevin Borlee Of Belgium Photo, 16; © SIHASAKPRACHUM/Shutterstock
Images, 19; © mezzotint/Shutterstock Images, 20; © Bvdc | Dreamstime.com - Athlete Photo, 22; © moodboard/
Thinkstock Images, 25; © Minerva Studio/Shutterstock Images, 27; © Pete Saloutos/Shutterstock Images, 28

Copyright ©2016 by Cherry Lake Publishing
All rights reserved. No part of this book may be reproduced or utilized in
any form or by any means without written permission from the publisher.

Library of Congress Cataloging-in-Publication Data

Labrecque, Ellen.
  The science of a sprint/Ellen Labrecque.
      pages cm.—(Full-Speed Sports)
  Includes bibliographical references and index.
  ISBN 978-1-63362-586-0 (hardcover)—ISBN 978-1-63362-766-6 (pdf)—ISBN 978-1-63362-676-8 (paperback)—
ISBN 978-1-63362-856-4 (ebook)
  1. Sprinting—Juvenile literature. 2. Sports sciences—Juvenile literature. I. Title.

  GV1069.L34 2015
  796.42'2—dc23
                                    2015005837

Cherry Lake Publishing would like to acknowledge the work of
the Partnership for 21st Century Skills. Please visit www.p21.org
for more information.

Printed in the United States of America
Corporate Graphics

ABOUT THE AUTHOR

Ellen Labrecque is a freelance writer living in Pennsylvania with her husband and two kids. She has written many non-fiction books and previously was an editor at *Sports Illustrated Kids* magazine. An avid runner, Ellen is always trying to figure out ways to become speedier.

TABLE OF CONTENTS

CHAPTER 1
The World's Fastest Man 4

CHAPTER 2
How Sprinting Started 10

CHAPTER 3
Super Sprinting Science 14

CHAPTER 4
The Pressure to Go Faster..................... 18

CHAPTER 5
How Fast Can We Go? 24

TIMELINE 29
THINK ABOUT IT 30
LEARN MORE 31
GLOSSARY 32
INDEX...32

THE WORLD'S FASTEST MAN

It is August 16, 2009, and athletes from across the globe are in Berlin, Germany, for the World Championships in Athletics. Sprinter Usain "Lightning" Bolt of Jamaica is in lane 4 racing in the 100-meter dash. Bolt wears his country's colors—green shorts and a gold top—on his massive frame. He stands at 6 feet 5 inches (195.5 centimeters) and weighs 207 pounds (94 kilograms), which is large for a sprinter. He is 6 inches (15 cm) taller than his American rival, Tyson Gay, who is racing in lane 5.

Bolt gives a quick wave to the crowd and settles down into his **starting blocks** on the bright-blue track. The starting gun is fired, and Bolt bursts out of the blocks like a rocket. He keeps his head down and then slowly raises it to look straight ahead. His arms are pumping back and forth as his stride stretches with every step. At about the 20-meter mark, Bolt takes a commanding lead over the seven other runners. By the 50-meter

Usain Bolt races in Berlin.

Usain Bolt begins his race in the 2008 Beijing Olympics.

Young runners race at the 2012 World Junior Athletics Championships.

mark, he is running at his top speed of 27.79 miles (44.7 kilometers) per hour.

Bolt crosses the finish line almost one full stride ahead of Gay, the second-place finisher. He glances at the clock next to the track, and his face lights up when he sees the numbers on the screen: 9.58 seconds. Bolt has set a new world record! He is officially the fastest man in the world. He grabs a Jamaican flag and carries it for a victory lap around the track. Photographers

Ryan Bailey and Usain Bolt were neck-and-neck in the 4x100 relay in the 2012 Summer Olympics.

snap pictures of his every move. The crowd stands and cheers wildly.

Four days later, Bolt sets a new world record in the 200-meter sprint of 19.19 seconds. At the 2012 Summer Olympics in London, England, Bolt wins gold medals in the 100- and 200-meter races. He and three teammates win gold and set another world record in the 4x100-meter relay of 36.84 seconds.

How did Bolt become the world's fastest man? How does he sprint so fast that he looks like he's flying? Let's look at the science behind sprinting.

THINK ABOUT IT!

On average, it takes most professional sprinters 44 steps to complete a 100-meter race. Usain Bolt completes the same distance in only 41. How does this give Bolt an advantage in a race?

CHAPTER 2

How Sprinting Started

Sprinting is running at top speed over a short distance. People have been racing each other since the beginning of time. But sprinting as an organized sport began with the first ancient Olympic Games in 776 BCE. In fact, it was the only event in these games. Racers sprinted across an approximately 200-meter course, called a stadion. Many of the competitors ran this race naked. They thought that would help them run faster.

The first ancient Olympic Games in Greece consisted entirely of sprinting races.

The last known ancient games were in 369 CE. It was another 1,500 years until the modern Olympic Games began, in 1896. At these games, sprinters ran a 100-meter and a 400-meter dash. Four years later, the 200-meter dash was added.

World records were first recorded in 1912. On July 6, 1912, Donald Lippincott of the United States ran the 100 meters in the record time of 10.6 seconds.

On the women's side, the first world record in the 100 meters was recorded on August 5, 1922, when Marie Mejzlikova II of Czechoslovakia ran the race in 13.6 seconds. Florence Griffith Joyner of the United States ran the 100 meters in 10.49 seconds in 1988 to set the current world record.

Most tracks have starting blocks for sprinters to practice with.

LOOK!

When sprinters begin a race, they start from a crouched position in a starting block. As they push off the block, this helps them **accelerate** faster than if they were standing up straight at the start. Why do you think this is the case?

CHAPTER 3

SUPER SPRINTING SCIENCE

The Olympic motto is made up of three Latin words: *Citius, altius, fortius,* meaning "faster, higher, stronger." Thanks to advancements in training—as well as in science, nutrition, and technology—sprinters are certainly getting faster and faster.

When sprinters begin a race, they want to get going quickly. A slow start can cost a runner any chance of winning. The use of starting blocks was first accepted in 1937 to help sprinters direct their initial pushes forward. Prior to this, some sprinters

A sprinter uses the starting block to push himself forward.

would dig a hole in the dirt track to help them generate a quick start.

When a sprinter is in the blocks, he is leaning forward with his hands on the track and his weight distributed across his body. Now, the sprinter's legs don't have to push up and lift his body. His legs can be used just to explode off the blocks with forward movement.

Once the sprinter gets going, he keeps his head down. Lifting his head right away would slow him down. All the momentum gained from pushing out of the blocks would go upward instead of toward the finish line.

Kevin Borlée has a sister and two brothers
who are also sprinting champions.

As the sprinter runs, he pumps his arms as hard as he can, not forcing his legs to do all the work. Sprinters usually reach their top speed at about 60 meters.

A runner's stride has two phases. The first is the stance phase, when one foot is hitting the ground. When the sprinter pushes off the track, the ground exerts force on the sprinter.

The flight phase of the stride is the second phase. This is when both feet are off the ground. A sprinter raises his knees high to stretch out each stride. He wants to cover as much space as he can before he hits the ground again.

Just before a sprinter finishes a race, he leans forward. This helps him cross the finish line as soon as possible.

THINK ABOUT IT!

Imagine that a sprinter gets off to a bad start from the starting block. What's one thing that could go wrong? What should the sprinter be more careful to do right next time?

CHAPTER 4

THE PRESSURE TO GO FASTER

Since the first modern Olympics, the sprint race has remained the same except for two key differences: the improvement in the running track and the improvement of athletic gear.

Synthetic tracks have played a major part in lowering sprint times. In the early Olympic Games, athletes ran on softer tracks made of crushed cinder, clay, or dirt. The last time an Olympic Games used a cinder track was in 1964 in Tokyo, Japan. Now, runners compete on a hard rubber-like surface. This makes them

*Tracks are made of hard but spongy material
that helps sprinters go faster.*

faster. Think about the difference between running on the sidewalk and running on the beach. A soft surface like sand or dirt steals the energy from a runner's legs and slows him down.

In the 1936 Olympics, world-famous sprinter Jesse Owens won the 100-meter race on a cinder track in 10.3 seconds. Modern scientists studied Owen's sprint speed and movement during this race. They determined that if Owen had run this race on today's synthetic surface, he would easily be as fast as today's sprinters.

Spikes help the sprinter's shoes grip the track.

[21ST CENTURY SKILLS LIBRARY]

Sprinters have also increased their speed thanks to tighter clothing and lighter shoes. Sprinters used to wear baggy shorts and shirts when they raced. But science revealed the importance of **aerodynamics** in sprinting. Now, sprinters wear form-fitting speed suits that keep the runner's profile as slim as possible. The Greek athletes in the ancient Olympic Games were onto something. These sleek uniforms help runners create less air resistance, a type of **friction**. The less air resistance, the faster a runner can go.

GO DEEPER!

Reread this section. What is the main idea? Considering all the advancements in technology, do you think sprinters from long ago could have been just as fast as sprinters today, even though their times were slower? Why or why not?

Besides the right shoes, a fast sprinter also needs the right form.

Lighter shoes have also helped athletes become speedier. Thanks to advanced technology, the spikes on a sprinter's shoes can weigh as little as 3 ounces (85 grams). This is the same weight as just three small envelopes. When sprinter Michael Johnson of the United States won gold medals in the 200- and 400-meter races at the 1996 Summer Olympics, his track spikes were so light they could only be used once. He went through six pairs on the way to his gold medals.

When sprinters in the early- to mid-1900s ran, their spiked sneakers were three times as heavy as today's shoes! The spikes were designed this way in part due to the old cinder tracks. When athletes ran on cinder tracks, they needed longer and heavier spikes to get more **traction** and to keep their feet from slipping.

These advances in technology help all sprinters. So, some competitors look for an extra edge to become the fastest in the world. This can come in the form of training and practicing harder than their competitors. But it can also lead sprinters to take dangerous drugs like **steroids** that help them become faster and stronger. Strict rules are in place to prevent athletes from using steroids. The hope is that all athletes will act with **integrity**, but it's also for the sake of their health. Steroid **abuse** can result in many unwanted physical effects, including baldness, acne, high blood pressure, liver cancer, or extra **aggression**.

CHAPTER 5

How Fast Can We Go?

Sprinters have never run as fast as 30 miles (48 km) per hour. With modern technology and the latest training techniques, reaching this speed might not be too far off.

Sprinters now use motion capturing technology to help them reach optimal speed. During motion capturing, sprinters put special reflective stickers all over themselves and then run in place on a treadmill. Computer sensors pick up these stickers and show an outline of the sprinter's moving form on a computer screen. Coaches and scientists can then

Record times keep getting faster and faster.

tweak the runner's arm or leg movements, to see if a slight change in form will help the athlete go faster.

Sprinters have also learned to train hard in the weight room, as well as on the track. In Jesse Owens' day, sprinters barely did weight training at all. Now, most Olympic-level sprinters spend at least 2 hours a day getting stronger in the weight room. Why? Strength and power lead to speed. The harder a sprinter hits the ground on each step, the faster he goes. Think of a super bouncy ball as having strong muscles and a soft, mushy beach ball as having weak muscles. The bouncy

GO DEEPER!

Reread this chapter so far. What are some exercises or stretches that you think would be helpful for sprinters? Go online to find out more.

Having a personalized workout can help a sprinter get faster and stronger.

Sprinting is a popular sport all over the world.

ball bounces right back and propels forward more easily. The soft beach ball hardly bounces at all.

Will a sprinter ever break 9 seconds in the 100 meters? Nobody knows for sure. But no matter how fast runners go, science is sure to play a role in the world's next record-breaking time.

[21ST CENTURY SKILLS LIBRARY]

TIMELINE

A TIMELINE HISTORY OF SPRINTING

776 BCE   The first ancient Olympic Games are held with runners sprinting 200 meters.

1896 CE   The first modern Olympics are held. Runners sprint in the 100- and 400-meter races.

1912   The first recorded world record for the men's 100-meter dash, 10.6 seconds, is set.

1922   The first recorded world record for the women's 100-meter dash, 13.6 seconds, is set.

1936   Jesse Owens of the United States wins four gold medals at the Olympics in Berlin, Germany, in the 100-, 200-, 400-, and 4x100-meter races.

1937   The use of the starting block is accepted in races.

1968   The Olympics in Mexico City, Mexico, become the first global track-and-field event on a firm synthetic surface.

1988   Florence Griffith Joyner of the United States sets the women's world record in the 100-meter dash with a time of 10.49 seconds.

2009   In a non-Olympic race, Usain Bolt of Jamaica sets the men's world record in the 100-meter dash with a time of 9.58 seconds.

2012   Usain Bolt wins the 100- and 200-meter race and is a member of the 4x100-meter winning team at the Summer Olympics in London, England. He sets a new Olympic record in the 100-meter with a time of 9.63 seconds.

THINK ABOUT IT

Think about what you knew about sprinting before reading this book. Did you learn any ways you can make yourself faster, now that you know the science behind it?

In chapter 4, you learned that the surface a sprinter runs on can help him go faster or slower. Do you think you could test this idea on your own? Try timing yourself running on grass. Then time yourself running the same distance on a hard surface. Which surface did you run faster on?

Do you think a human will someday be able to run faster than a cheetah? Why or why not?

[21ST CENTURY SKILLS LIBRARY]

LEARN MORE

FURTHER READING

Bloom, Marc. *Young Runners: The Complete Guide to Healthy Running for Kids from 5 to 18*. New York: Simon & Schuster, 2009.

Goodrow, Carol. *Kids Running: Have Fun, Get Faster, and Go Farther*. Halcottsville, NY: Breakaway Books, 2008.

Savage, Jeff. *Usain Bolt*. Minneapolis: Lerner, 2013.

WEB SITES

Bleacher Report—Top 50 United States Olympic Track and Field Moments
http://bleacherreport.com/articles/1191416-top-50-united-states-olympic-track-and-field-moments
Check out this slideshow of some incredible Olympic track and field performances.

Healthy Kids Running Series—Location
http://www.healthykidsrunningseries.org/race-calendar/locations/
Learn about a kids' running program, and see if there's a race happening nearby that you could join.

International Association of Athletics Federations
www.iaaf.org
This site lets readers stay updated on all world track-and-field news, including world records.

GLOSSARY

abuse (uh-BYOOS) wrong or harmful use of something, such as steroids

accelerate (ak-SEL-uh-rate) to move or go faster, or change velocity's direction

aerodynamics (air-oh-dye-NAM-iks) the branch of science that studies the effects of air—whether slowing down or speeding up—on people or things in motion

aggression (uh-GRESH-uhn) violent or threatening behavior

friction (FRIK-shuhn) the resistance when two things rub together, like wind against a sprinter

integrity (in-TEG-ri-tee) the quality of being honest and having high moral principles

starting blocks (STAHR-ting BLAHKS) rigid blocks that sprinters push off against at the start of a race to help them start running more quickly

steroids (STER-oydz) types of drugs that can make a person faster, stronger, or bigger; some have dangerous side effects and are illegal

synthetic tracks (sin-THET-ik TRAKS) spongy surfaces that encourage extreme speeds

traction (TRAK-shuhn) a type of friction that keeps a runner from slipping

INDEX

aerodynamics, 21

Bolt, Usain "Lightning," 4–9

clothing, 21
crouched position, 13

flight phase, 17
forward lean, 15, 17

gear, 18, 21–23

momentum, 15

pumping arms, 5, 17

resistance, air, 21

shoes, 21, 22–23
speed, 7, 12, 17, 19, 24–28
spikes, 20, 22–23
sprinting
    history, 10–13

stance phase, 17
starting blocks, 5, 13, 14–15
steroids, 23
stride, 5, 17

track, 18–19
training, 23, 24–28

[21ST CENTURY SKILLS LIBRARY]